Hacking

2016 Computer Hacking Guide for Beginners

Computer Hacking,How to Hack,Basic Security, Computer Systems

by James Clark

Table of Contents

Hacking

2016 Computer Hacking Guide for Beginners

Table of Contents

Introduction

Chapter 1 – A Brief History of Hacking

Chapter 2 – Cybersecurity Basics

Chapter 3 – Enter the White Hats

Chapter 4 – How to Become a White Hat

Chapter 5 – Where to work as a White Hat

Chapter 6 – Charitable White Hats

Conclusion

Disclaimer

While all attempts have been made to verify the information provided in this book, the author does not assume any responsibility for errors, omissions, or contrary interpretations of the subject matter contained within. The information provided in this book is for educational and entertainment purposes only. The reader is responsible for his or her own actions and the author does not accept any responsibilities for any liabilities or damages, real or perceived, resulting from the use of this information.

Introduction

Hacking is a term that means different things to different people. For some, it means a person who pushes a system or device far beyond its limits or adapts it to uses that were not intended.

Do a google search for Kinetic, Microsoft's motion control gaming technology. Seeing the numerous ways this one technology has been hacked to be used for everything from building a virtual dressing room to creating a lightsaber wielding robot arm will illustrate the point perfectly.

On the other hand, the word "hacker" is synonymous with "criminal" in the minds of many. And just as the creative modifier interpretation has plenty of evidence to back it up, there is plenty of evidence to back up the criminal interpretation as well.

Nearly every daywe hear of some company or institution getting hacked in some fashion. Whether it is Target or LinkedIn suffering a security breach with thousands of customers' data being compromised or the recent rash of hospitals getting hit with ransomware, there are plenty of reasons why hackers are almost universally seen as the bad guys, or "black hats" – a term borrowed from old black-and-white westerns.

Yet, these are not the only images we have of hackers in the popular consciousness. From movies like *Hackers* in the 1990's and the more recent Blackhat to comic books where the character of Oracle regularly helps Batman and others defeat the forces evil with her extensive hacking skills, hackers are often portrayed as protectors.

These are cultural representations of a new breed of hacker, the "white hat," who uses her knowledge of computers and programming not for personal gain but to help protect the institutions they work for, and often the public at large from the attacks of their more nefarious black hat counterparts.

With the aforementioned rise in cybercrime has come an increased focus on cybersecurity for individuals and institutions, leading to an ever increasing demand for white hats to head up cyber security and test their own systems to expose weaknesses befor they can be exploited.

This guide will provide you a brief overview of the history of hacking, a review of basic cybersecurity procedures, and how to become a white hat.

At the end, you will find a list of resources that will help you find a place to get certified, learn about hacking conventions and understand some of the terminology that we'll be throwing around pretty loosely in this guide.

Chapter 1 – A Brief History of Hacking

Hacking has been around at least since the 1960's when the term was coined in reference to a group of MIT students who spent time modifying their train sets and eventually went on to apply that same mindset to modifying the new computers that were beginning to be available.

Those positive connotations faded when the next decade brought on the rise of the "phreak." Phreaks were people who hacked the phone system in some way. This brand of hacker got their start when John Draper used a toy whistle to imitate a tone necessary for making long distance calls.

Using this trick, Draper and others like him were able to make free long distance calls. Many went farther and built "blue boxes." These were devices that nearly anyone could use to hack the phone system. Two of the earliest builders of these blue boxes were none other than Steve Jobs and Steve Wozniak, the founders of Apple Computers.

Hacking didn't strongly gain mainstream awareness until the movie *Wargames* was released. This film featured a high school student who hacked his way into a computer that was tied into all of the military's decision making systems, specifically those governing the launch of nuclear missiles.

Naturally, the main character nearly started World War III.

In the meantime, most real world hackers were busy exploring various electronic systems, curious to see how they worked and what they might be capable of beyond their original design.

These hackers were motivated by a desire to explore the world around them, to dig deep into their systems and play around for the sheer joy of the task.

Unfortunately, they were overshadowed by those who would use the relatively open access of nearly all the computer systems in North America for their own personal gain, such as financial rewards for delivering information, ransoms for not destroying systems are simply prestige with the rest of the hacking community.

Because of this, new laws began to come into effect, criminalizing behavior that had previously been acceptable and putting the brakes on the early golden-age of hacking.

During the 1990's the Internet began to enter the mainstream, and with it, fears of identity and credit card theft, as well as computer viruses that could turn a thousand dollar machine into a useless pile of transistors.

This also marked the first major increase in Information Technology (IT) professionals and departments dedicated not only to making sure that a given institution's computers worked correctly but also to protect them from outside attack.

The black hats struck again with phishing and social engineering scams. If you remember the classic, "I am a Nigerian prince" emails, then you know exactly what these terms mean.

Essentially, an email would be sent outlining a plan by which a given person would be selected to help out said prince (or general) by holding some money in your bank account for a short period of time, after which the person would be granted a substantial reward.

Naturally all that was needed was your account information. It is surprising how many people fell for this simple trick and how many people fall for similar tricks today.

These days, there are a whole host of threats from various kinds of hackers. Malware, spyware, worms and other code designed to cause harm abound. Each of these can bring down your home computer if you are not careful and even wreak havoc on a better protected corporate system.

The credible while hat will be able to protect his system against most attacks and also simulate attacks on the system, testing to see how far he can penetrate his own employer's hard drives and networks.

Chapter 2 – Cybersecurity Basics

If you are going to hook up any device, whether a desktop computer loaded with 4 terabytes of storage and 32 gigabytes of RAM or a smartphone, it is important to understand certain basic does and don'ts of cybersecurity.

First and foremost, get some kind of anti-virus software. McCafee and Norton are still the most popular programs on the market. There are better options though, which is a good thing, as McCafee and Norton have both been described as malware by users in the past due to the tendency of those programs to adversely affect the performance of systems they are installed on.

Kaspersky and Avast are both other mainstream anti-virus programs that have a far better reputation for providing quality protection without excessively bogging down your system.

Speaking of bogging things down, there are also your firewall settings to consider. There are numerous security settings within a standard firewall program, ranging from "let everything through" to "stop it all, in fact, just don't even bother putting me online."

As you can imagine, neither of those extremes is particularly useful. One provides no protection and the other pretty much stops you from getting anything done at all. There will be settings in the middle and even the ability to customize so that you can decide what does and does not get through your system automatically, what you have to give specific permission for, and what does get blocked by default.

Good Practices

Whether you are a system administrator or an individual user, there are certain basic cybersecurity practices you should do and encourage others on the network to practice.

Chief among these is updating your software. No matter how well any piece of software is written, there will always be weaknesses that can be exploited and they are constantly being uncovered by black hats taking advantage of them, in-house white hats whose job it is to find them and independent groups of white hats who regularly test programs and websites as something of a public service.

Once these exploits are uncovered, the relevant company will quickly develop a patch to fix them. Such patches will be delivered via software updates.

These patches are completely useless if you don't regularly update the software. Fortunately, it is simple enough to set up automatic updates to ensure that you are never more than a week behind on the latest patches.

All anti-virus programs also come with the ability to scan for viruses and other vulnerabilities in your system. Yes, the program should stop any viruses from getting onto your servers or individual drives but a hastily given permission or thoughtlessly downloaded bit of malware can still result in holes in your security. A full scan should identify these holes and allow you to eliminate them with little effort.

A system admin should make a habit of reviewing the firewall's logs to see what sort of attacks are being made against the network. Repeated attacks from the same IP address, on the same area of the network or the same type of attack can be indicative of an attempt to target your network for criminal activity.

It is important to distinguish between actual attempts to hack the network and relatively harmless scans as chasing down every single person who makes an untoward pass at the network is a poor use of limited time and resources.

Be careful what you download and where you download it from. If you see that latest edition of Photoshop for $5 from a site called Steve's Stupendous Deals, it would be wise to stay away. If a deal seems too good to be true, it almost certainly is.

Even downloading from reputable sites like CNET can be tricky as they like to tack on additional programs to the one you are actually trying to get. While this software may be benign, it will bog down your system and likely come with their down security flaws, opening you up to whole new lines of attack.

Email is a favorite means of attack for hackers. In addition to the infamous Nigerian prince emails mentioned above, black hats will attempt to trick people into downloading a virus by sending an email while posing as someone from your contacts list.

These emails can come with attachments that seem to be a nice family photo but in fact contain software that will compromise your system. More recently, such attacks will not even require that you download an attachment, only that you open the email.

Phishing for your personal financial data has also gotten more sophisticated in recent years as well, with hackers sending emails that purport to be from your bank, Amazon or some other online entity that you regularly do business with requesting you to verify credit card or account numbers due to a security breach.

Yes, hackers do have a sense of humor while they are getting ready to fleece your savings. They will even include links to very official looking websites that can easily lead a casual observer into thinking they are legitimate.

Look for misspelled words, differences in the logo and other tell tales such as whether or not there is more to the site than the page you are currently on.

Another basic way of protecting your financial data is to make sure that you never do any buying or selling while on a public computer or network. Properly equipped hackers can pick out passwords and other data being transmitted from your device to the network's router.

Having a good password may well be the most obvious security step to take but it is amazing just how many people ignore this. Plenty of people choose something simple like "123456" or "password." These are not clever. What they are is insanely easy to crack.

Do not choose these, or something like "login," or your kids' names, or your favorite hobby. Anyone who knows you and for some reason wants to get into your system will start by guessing these first. Even if no one who knows you tries to crack your password, another hacker might decide to try it and will seek to gather such information from your social media accounts.

 If those accounts are open to the public, there will be plenty of information available to develop a list of likely passwords.

There are also hackers who will utilize bot-nets to attack your password, using dedicated logarithms to eventually break through. There are a couple of simple steps to take to either defeat or at least frustrate such systems. One is to ensure your system will lock out any login attempts after a certain number of tries. The other is to seek to improve the password itself.

Recent studies have shown that following a few simple steps will result in a far more secure password.

- Sixteen characters long
- One number
- One special character
- At least one capital letter
- Begin and end with a letter

Yes, you will definitely need to write these passwords down and keep them in a secure location. But it is definitely worth it as this criteria combines into a format that is difficult for the bot-nets to crack. And as difficult as it may be to believe, if you login at least once a day, eventually, you will remember the password within a couple of weeks.

Naturally, the security of this format is likely to change so be sure to keep up with best practices by following security websites and forums.

Finally, when online, do not click on any pop-ups, no matter how official or enticing they look. Pop-ups are a favorite way for hackers to trick people into downloading various kinds of malicious software.

Chapter 3 – Enter the White Hats

After spending all that time talking about some of the many ways that hackers will attempt to steal your data or that of your employer, you may be a little nervous and paranoid about the term again, having flashbacks to the movie *The Net* in which Sandra Bullock has her identity stolen by malicious hackers.

Remember, not all hackers, not even most, are of this criminal sort. The original usage of the term, applied to people who are engaged in nothing more than pushing various systems to their limit, still obtains for most. The closest thing to a crime most hackers commit is voiding their factory warranties.

Then there are the white hats, hackers who engage in many of the same activities that black hats do but do it with the intent of exposing flaws in cybersecurity and repairing them before they can exposed by those who would exploit those flaws and cause a great deal of damage in the process.

We'll now spend some time talking about what these white hats actually do, how to become one and what sort of jobs are available once you get certified.

What do they actually do?

White hats are also known as penetration testers. As it turns out, that is actually a very descriptive name as many of them spend their days testing how easy it is to penetrate a given network.

They do this by using the same sort of methods as a criminal hacker. DNS attacks, phishing, social engineering, using botnets to crack a password are daily activities for a penetration tester.

Once inside, it is the job of the tester to see how far into the network she can get and what kind of damage she can do. The tester of course is not doing any damage herself, only seeing what would be possible if a less well-intentioned hacker had broken in.

Naturally, the job is not all poking around in the bowels of computer networks. Once the test is complete, a report must be made, outlining any discovered vulnerabilities with recommendations on how to fix them.

Chapter 4 – How to Become a White Hat

There is no clearly defined path for becoming a white hat. Clearly, you should have a love for computers, a passion for security and have the ability to solve problems creatively and perhaps most of all, think like the enemy. However, while there is no step-by-step process, there are certain things that you can do to increase the likelihood of getting hired as an ethical hacker.

A logical first step is to get a cybersecurity degree. This was once merely a part of the broader IT degree but with the growth of cyberwarfare and cybercrime it has become a field unto its own. There are a number of colleges and universities, online and on campus that offer bachelors and masters degrees in this field.

Some, such as Utica College and Lewis University have been recognized by the National Security Agency (NSA) for the quality of their cybersecurity programs. Another option is the National Cyberwatch Center which can help you get a two-year associates degree that will transfer to another college to get a bachelor's degree in another two years.

Finally, there is always the military. The military will provide training, experience and if you live in the United States, money for further education in cybersecurity in the form of the GI Bill.

Beyond getting a degree, there are a number of certifications that are worth getting that will help you get hired. Among the most prominent of these is the Certified Ethical Hacker (CEH) certification given by the International Council of E-commerce Consultants (EC-Council).

The EC-Council's CEH course is an accredited course that teaches students to get into the mind of a hacker, teaching them the five phases of hacking for ethical hackers and using labs that mimic real life scenarios, allowing them to learn many of the technologies and techniques that real hackers use to accomplish their ends.

There are a number of other courses offered by the EC-Council as well, ranging from two-day certificates like Wireless Safety and Threats and Defense Mechanisms to longer five day certification courses such as the CEH course mentioned above and others like Certified Security Analyst and their highest level certification, Licensed Penetration Tester.

Comptia is also a highly reputable certification organization. They provide study guides and courses for several levels of IT professional, going from the entry level A+ certification,

Network admin, and finally to the globally recognized Security+ certification. Their prices are not nearly as affordable as Udemy (more on that below) but they are considerably less than those provided by the EC-Council and are still recognized around the world for the quality and thoroughness of their training.

Other options to consider are certifications from the Information Systems Audit and Control Association (ISACA), the Global Information Assurance Certification (GIAC), and the International Information Systen Certification Consortium (ISC2). All are highly reputable and recognized world wide and will help you as you begin you career in cybersecurity.

A little investigation will reveal that most of these courses, while highly reputable, are also very expensive. A more affordable option is Udemy, which provides a number of related online courses for $50 dollars or less. These likely will not get you the best paying jobs, but they will help you get your foot in the door.

You may also have noticed that these certificates and certifications don't take very long. That should be a clear indicator that these are not the equivalent of college courses and will be assuming a certain base level of knowledge before you even sign up. Which bring us to the other, and most important aspect of becoming a professional white hat – experience.

As we said earlier, there is no defined path towards becoming a white hat. Degrees and certifications will absolutely help you but there is no substitute for having already worked in the cybersecurity world.

In fact, the EC-Council requires that you have two years of security experience before taking their course. So, how do you get that experience without the shiny certifications and certificates propping up your resume?

This is where it really pays to be patient. And also very self-directed. Barring experienced gained through military service, you can earn a basic A+ certification and then search out any IT job that is available, whether it is software engineering, network administrator or even web development.

The important thing is that it is a foot in the door. Once you have gotten a good job in the IT world, work your way into a security related position, earning whatever certifications that are available to you.

Many companies will either provide their own training or offer tuition reimbursement for you to increase your knowledge and skill set. After all, this benefits the company at least as much as it will benefit you.

Attend as many conferences and events such as DEF CON or a local hackathon as you are able so that you can network with other industry professionals. More than one job has been landed simply because of knowing the right person and being in the right place at the right time. Always seek to either move up in your organization or to a more prominent one.

Some of the best cybersecurity conferences for both education and networking are:

DEF CON

– This is the grandfather of cybersecurity conferences. Begun by hacking legend Dark Tangent in 1993 and held every year in Las Vegas, DEF CON is a must to attend at some point in your career as a cybersecurity professional.

It has become a clearing house of ideas and techniques for improving the security of everything from corporate servers to insulin pumps. It doesn't stop there though as there is also a wide range of hardware hacks present as well. No matter your favorite technological hobby, you are sure to find something of interest at DEF CON.

Black Hat –

The name Black Hat is a bit misleading here. Rather than being a gathering of illegal hackers, it is, like its older brother DEF CON, a must attend for cybersecurity professionals.

The conference was also begun by Dark Tangent and is the more corporate friendly version of the older and slightly more well-known convention. This gathering places a lot of emphasis on cybersecurity training.

It also is the place to go to be the first to hear about the latest security vulnerabilities, with a gag put on many presenters for months after the conference so that the vulnerabilities can be fixed before falling into the hands of actual black hats.

Schmoocon –

This is a bit more affordable than some other conferences. But don't worry, you are still getting high quality as the organizers are some of the best hackers in the business (Linux Apache is on their list of accomplishments) and they make sure they recruit only high quality presenters.

Toorcon –

In addition to being a great convention and a good place to start your career in cybersecurity due to its intimate, 400 attendee maximum, it also takes things beyond the con and organizes camps and world tours, events that are often held in somewhat out of the way, but very interesting locations.

You can also practice your skills on your own. No, I don't mean start trying to crack networks and infect other systems. That would be illegal and could land you in jail, which certainly won't help you get a job. Rather, try to crack your own network. Set up your router and firewalls in different configurations and practice bypassing them.

Add-ons and apps like Firesheep and Droidsheep are free and useful in helping you practice your skills by cracking into your own accounts. Hack this Site will allow you to practice hacking into websites.

 Applying your skills in this way will help you refine them and prevent you from forgetting whatever you learn in your courses if it should for some reason take you longer than you would like to land a job in cybersecurity. They will also go a long way to ensuring that you are able to pass any practical tests that are required as part of a company's hiring process.

Equally important is that you never stop learning. Cybersecurity is one of the fastest changing jobs in the world right now, with operating systems constantly developing, new anti-virus programs coming on the market and hackers constantly trying to find new ways to subvert them, you cannot afford to stand still.

Those events and conferences will be invaluable in this, as will keeping up with various tech forums and publications.

Is it worth it?

With all of the time, effort, and money that goes into getting the most sought-after qualifications and in keeping up with such a fluid industry, is it really worth pursuing this as a career?

First, the chances are that if you are considering it already, you need to have love for the work. If you enjoy tinkering with computer systems and spending time immersed in lines and lines of code that would be indecipherable to most mere mortals, then this is definitely for you.

Second, this is a rapidly growing field. That ever growing list of companies and governments that have been the victims of attacks of various kinds has sent the industry scrambling to increase their defenses. This fact is one of the reasons that degrees and certifications are not strictly necessary.

There simply are not enough candidates with those defined qualifications for companies to hire.

This has led to many beginning to break from what has been the norm over the last several decades of requiring some sort of piece of paper before believing that a candidate can do the job.

They are going back to the older method of judging a person based on demonstrated merit and interviews run by people who are already knowledgeable about the job to determine if the candidate has what it takes.

All of that demand also affects wages. The lowest an ethical hacker should expect to make is $50,000 a year at entry level. After just a few years, a certified ethical hacker can command upwards of $100,000. And wages are likely to continue increasing in the years to come.

So yes, if you love working with computers and diving into the code, the hard work and patience needed to be successful as a professional white hat are definitely worth it.

Chapter 5 – Where to work as a White Hat

Any moderately sized company or organization is going to have at least one IT professional on staff. However, if you want to make the kind of money discussed above, you will need to go a little bigger.

Banks, credit firms, department stores, online retailers and even movie studios are all in need of dedicated cybersecurity professionals to keep their data and that of their customers safe from prying eyes.

Software developers are also in need of talent to help develop the next generation of cyber defenses, patching existing software, hunting and killing viruses and developing encryption that will keep the black hats at bay.

Governments make extensive use of ethical hackers as well. The applications here are numerous, from defending government networks from cyberattacks, developing and cracking encryption, attacking terrorist networks and developing new software to gain an advantage on the cyber-battlefield.

Yet another area of interest is computer forensics. Government intelligence agencies and police departments have begun to make more use of hackers to investigate cybercrime and track down the perpetrators.

This more specialized field of ethical hacking requires a private investigator license in some states (if operating independently of a law enforcement agency) and requires a more extensive knowledge of the laws pertaining to cybercrime and how to obtain a search warrant.

Finally, you can always get hired by a private cybersecurity firm. The activities that you would be engaged in would vary from firm to firm but could include any or all of the above.

Chapter 6 – Charitable White Hats

Do ethical hackers really exist? Certainly. Do they exist outside of a defined institution where they get a paycheck for their efforts? In short, are there hackers who use their talents for more charitable causes as well? Naturally, the answer is "yes."

One of the most notable examples is the Molengeek initiative. Started in Molenbeek, the same neighborhood that spawned the terrorists responsible for the 2016 terror attacks in Brussels, Molengeek aims to give talented young hackers a way to develop and showcase their skills while at the same time keeping them away from recruiters for Islamic extremist groups.

And as you may recall, first responders to the attacks were plagued by communications problems, problems that the young hackers of Molengeek are solving by developing apps specific to the task.

Code for America is another ethical hacking group that is helping to improve resource management in municipalities across the United States. Citizen volunteers are helping improve data analysis, resident safety and more through the use of open source software.

Jay Radcliffe is a name known to many in the white hat world. Radcliffe is a diabetic who wondered if his internet connected insulin pump could be hacked and what it could be made to do.

What he found was more than a little disquieting and turned him into a villain in the eyes of many – the pumps could actually be hacked and be remotely instructed to deliver a dose of insulin that could kill the pump's user.

The findings were so significant that the United States Congress ordered an investigation into the vulnerabilities of other medical equipment, including internet connected pacemakers.

Other examples abound and include demonstrations of hacking ATMs, getting the doors on a Tesla to open, putting extra money on a subway card and more. It should be noted that white hats who bring these issues to light often become the target of lawsuits for their work in exposing security threats.

However, since they do so with the intent of finding and showing off these flaws before the black hats do in the hopes that they will be fixed, these prosecutions rarely go anywhere.

Conclusion

Hopefully, after this brief overview, you will be convinced that you don't have to be a criminal to be a hacker. You don't even have to start out as a criminal and then reform after an offer from the government like in the movies.

The disquieting – and exciting – truth is that cybercrime is on the rise, with the malicious black hat hackers growing more sophisticated by the day and to counter them, companies are increasingly willing to pay top dollar for talented white hats to build up their defenses.

And if defense isn't your thing, you can get a job with the government to go on the offense against the black hats and terrorists, stopping them before they can even act.

If you follow the advice in this guide and pursue the recommended education and certifications, you can find yourself with a profitable and rewarding career in cybersecurity.

Resources

Certifications

https://www.isc2.org/

http://www.isaca.org/about-isaca/Pages/default.aspx

http://www.giac.org/

https://www.eccouncil.org/

https://www.udemy.com/

Conventions

https://www.defcon.org/

https://www.blackhat.com/

https://shmoocon.org/

https://toorcon.net/

General

Helpful list of colleges and universities with solid cybersecurity degree programs.

http://www.cyberdegrees.org/listings/

Don't understand a word that was said? Here's a helpful glossary.

https://evestigate.com/cyber-crime-hacker-terms-to-know/

Hackers doing good.

http://molengeek.com/

https://www.codeforamerica.org/